W9-CBR-880

Freethinking Mystics With Hands

Exploring the Heart of Unitarian Universalism

Tom Owen-Towle

Skinner House Books
Boston

Published by Skinner House Books. Skinner House Books is
an imprint of the Unitarian Universalist Association, a liberal
religious organization with more than 1,000 congregations in
the U.S. and Canada. 25 Beacon Street, Boston, MA 02108-
2800.

Printed in the USA.

ISBN 1-55896-367-7

Cataloging in Publication Data is on file with the publisher.

10 9 8 7 6 5 4 3
05 04 03

Unitarian Universalists covenant
to affirm and promote:

The inherent worth and dignity of every person

Justice, equity, and compassion in human relations

Acceptance of one another and encouragement to spiritual growth in our congregations

A free and responsible search for truth and meaning

The right of conscience and the use of the democratic process within our congregations and in society at large

The goal of world community with peace, liberty, and justice for all

Respect for the interdependent web of all existence of which we are a part.

Contents

Introduction

Unitarian Universalists aspire to be an intentionally diverse and inclusive religious enterprise. Consequently, our history has contained a Joseph Priestley, who discovered wisdom through the empirical avenue of science; a Margaret Fuller, whose transcendentalism honored interior communion with the divine; a William Ellery Channing, who claimed reason as the central doorway to spiritual enlightenment; and a Clara Barton, who found transformation via loving service. Unitarian Universalism is spacious enough to include all such exemplars of wisdom plus others who might choose distinct or composite sacred routes.

My particular version of the Unitarian Universalist way of religion exhorts us to live reasonably, intuitively, and compassionately during our one precious span of days and nights. Amplifying a phrase from the religious activist Daniel Berrigan, "O God, send us mystics with hands," I would characterize us as *free-thinking mystics with hands*!

First, the freethinking component of Unitarian Universalism challenges us to pay homage to reason—a virtue that brings a clarifying, steadying influence in a world that prizes the impetuous and flamboyant. Reason entails the readiness to look before leaping, to ponder an issue and attach due weight to each side, to view things not through distorted or magnifying lenses, but, as far as possible, as they truly are.

In an era when cults are rampant and irrationality is pervasive, the Unitarian Universalist way of religion declares that our human minds are sacred gifts to be fully engaged. Kurt Vonnegut warns an American society increasingly in revolt against rationality: "If you want to be unloved and forgotten, be reasonable!"

After all, who wants to practice the daily rigors of reflection when tempted to glide on the wings of the latest mindless fad? Naturally, we all have occasional zany moments. As one wit remarked, "Every one of us should be a damn fool for at least five minutes every day. Wisdom simply consists in not exceeding that limit."

Unitarian Universalists belong to a heritage that holds tenaciously to the value of reasonableness, what parish minister Duncan Howlett, in his book *The Critical Way in Religion*, describes as follows:

> The critical way is the way of those who believe the certainty offered by the religions is unobtainable by anyone. We believe that ultimate questions must of necessity have open-ended answers.

Freethinkers ardently believe in the worth, not the in-fallibility, of human reason. Hence, Unitarian Univer-salism is not a religion of reason, where reason is the noun, the substance. Rather, Unitarian Universalism is a reasonable religion, where freethinking prevails as an adjective or modifier. We use our reason to the fullest to explore but not capture life's inescapable mysteries.

Unitarian Universalists are suspicious of that which is felt but unprovable, insistently real but not intellec-tually grasped. It is often difficult for us to confess that we dwell in a universe utterly beyond our creation, our control, and even our comprehension.

Yet our mystical bent would posit unequivocally: "There is so much we do not know that remains mys-terious. We are sustained by processes and powers that we can neither fathom nor do without. The universe is wondrously, terrifyingly inexplicable. And we like it that way." Listen to the sentiments of Jacob Trapp, a preeminent Unitarian Universalist mystic, from his book *Return to the Springs:*

> I like to think of mysticism as the art of meet-ing reality, the art of richer and deeper awareness. It is an experience that comes unbidden . . . it is not the intellectual convic-tion that Being itself is my being, but rather an ineffable experience of that Oneness, flood-ing in to overwhelm our illusion of aloneness, separateness. There are moments when life

seems vivid and resplendent, when a more than mortal splendor breaks in, when there is a touch of grandeur and of glory in just being alive.

Most of us have had, however modest or irregular, transrational moments of union with self, neighbor, nature, or God that we might designate as mystical epiphanies. These numinous encounters cannot be adequately verbalized. They impel us to song, silence, or often tears. They drive us to our knees or to leaping with joy. Unitarian Universalism is a reasonable faith that pushes the mind as far as it can go, before bowing to the mysteries of birth and death, solitude and sexuality, evil and goodness.

We consummate our Unitarian Universalist religious journey through the employment of our hands. Ultimately, we are measured not by our reasonable thoughts or hallowed encounters but rather by the breadth of our justice-building and peace-making. We extend our hands in hospitality to the stranger and the marginalized. We handle church conflicts in honorable fashion. We dirty our hands in messy social causes. We join hands in friendship and love. We lift our hands in celebration. We raise our hands in protest. And, yes, we wring our hands in frustration and anguish.

Ever-informed minds and transformed souls must reform the worlds wherein we dwell. Hence, we are beckoned to meditate and march, pray and protest, commune with nature and clean up our streets, raise hell and experience heaven—be freethinking mystics with hands. Biblical testaments offer renderings of our Unitarian Universalist imperative: "Thou shalt love the Lord thy God with all thy *soul* (the mystical enterprise), and with all thy *mind* (the gift of rationality), and with all thy *strength* (the power of enactment)."

Unitarian Universalists are freethinkers: unfettered pilgrims in search of governing truths. We are mystics as well: spiritually attuned to marvels of the universe and awake to omens of the divine. We are also blessed with hands outstretched in praise, resistance, and caring embrace. Holding fast to our mission as freethinking mystics with hands, Unitarian Universalism will transform individual lives while shaping the moral contours of the world as it moves into the twenty-first century!

Acquaintance With the Depths

The old watchwords of liberalism—freedom, reason and tolerance—worthy though they be, are simply not catching the imagination of the contemporary world. They describe a process for approaching the religious depths, but they testify to no intimate acquaintance with the depths themselves. If we are ever to speak to a new age, we must supplement our seeking with some profound religious findings.

—O. Eugene Pickett
UUA Presidential Address, 1979

The leading principles of Unitarian Universalism—freedom, reason, and tolerance—are instrumental values rather than terminal ones. They are effective vehicles for engaging life's depths and enabling us to create transformative communities of hope and love. Ralph Waldo Emerson, in his Divinity School Address of 1838, articulated the same vision when he said to unseasoned ministers: "Yourself a newborn bard of the Holy Ghost, cast behind you all conformity, and acquaint people at first hand with Deity!"

The key word for both Emerson and O. Eugene Pickett is *acquaintance*. It means more than exposure, is different from mastery. Acquaintance resembles what Jewish philosopher Martin Buber called *meeting*. He once remarked: "I said we believe; I mean, of course, we meet!" Buber maintained that the religious struggle requires soulful encounter, what the Psalmist referred to as "deep calling unto deep."

Freethinkers are often caricatured as drowning in lofty abstractions, while mystics are depicted as lost in metaphysical mist. As freethinking mystics at our finest, Unitarian Universalists navigate the depths rather than the shallows of religion firsthand, be it through the senses, intuition, or reason. We employ our eyes and ears, composing principles truthful to our core commitments and to our caring of others. Buddha's watchword was *ehipassiko*, which translates: "Come, see for yourself!"

Religion has been associated predominantly with height imagery. Its theology, its standards of morality, its architecture are all portrayed as remote and thrusting heavenward. But Unitarian Universalists ardently disagree. We underscore the view expressed by Sophia Fahs in *Today's Children and Yesterday's Heritage*:

> The religious way is the deep way . . . the way that dips into the heart of things . . . that sees what physical eyes alone fail to see, the intangibles at the heart of every phenomenon.

The Gospel of Luke offers us a story about the depths. After a frustrating night of fruitless labor, Peter and his companions are cleaning their nets in preparation for going home. Suddenly, Jesus appears on the bank, just off shore, teaching the crowd. As they push in on him, Jesus gets into Peter's boat and asks him to pull out a little from the shore. Then Jesus directs Peter to "put out into deep water and spread out your nets for a catch." Peter initially resists Jesus' request: "Master, we worked hard all night long and caught nothing." Peter eventually relents: ". . . but if you say so, I will spread out the nets." They then catch such a huge number of fish that their nets begin to tear. They call their companions to come help with a second boat, and the final catch fills both boats nearly to the sinking point.

Jesus' invitation to drop our nets into the depths can be seen as an overture to a more profound exploration of our souls. We are sorely frightened to leave the surfaces of existence and to delve downward into consciousness and growth. Yet Unitarian Universalist religion is relentless in beckoning us to climb down from elevated perches, to vacate the comfortable surrounds of life's surface, and to enter life's depths where authentic suffering, joy, and meaning await us.

Children of Heresy

Each human is confronted not by a single occasion, a single choosing, but by unpunctuated choosing. Among the myriad decisions none stands aside. In a lifetime of choice, a nationtime of choice, each matters!
—Rudolph Nemser

The word "heresy" is actually a respectable term, at least by definition. It is derived from the Greek word meaning "to choose." Unitarian Universalists contend that "choice"—not inheritance, fate, or default—determines the nature of one's religion. We belong to the heritage of incorrigible choice-makers, an admirable lineage of heretics from Michael Servetus to Susan B. Anthony, from Benjamin Rush to Olympia Brown, from Whitney Young Jr. to Sophia Fahs.

Let's amble back in history and revisit the "Religious Toleration and Freedom of Conscience" edict issued at the Diet of Torda in 1568 by King John Sigismund of Transylvania. The crux of this decree stated that "No one shall be reviled for their religion by anyone," encouraging all to hold fast to the directives of their own consciences. The language is clearly sixteenth century, but the message rings valid for the waning days of the twentieth century, when many throughout the world are reviled, or even killed, for their religion.

On the contrary, our Unitarian Universalist ancestors argued that religion must remain unconstrained, that in questions of faith there is no place for compulsion or conformity, only free choice. It is notable that during the only time in history that a Unitarian government held sway (late sixteenth-century Transylvania), it immediately used its power not to oppress other forms of religion or to secure exceptional privilege for its own adherents, but to insist upon equal rights and benefits for all.

This groundbreaking decree of religious freedom in the Western world saluted every person as an equal pilgrim on life's sacred path. Furthermore, this bedrock principle was expressed by the sixteenth-century Unitarian Francis Dávid in language that still applies today: "We are not to *think* alike but to *love* alike."

Freedom of conscience is a deceptively radical notion signaling that neither homeland nor deity comes first in individual lives, but our conscience does. Naturally, human consciences do not operate in a vacuum. They need to be clarified by the loving critique of fellow truth-seekers. We must decide for ourselves what to believe and do, but never solely by ourselves. As writer Albert Camus argued in *The Rebel*:

All people and all sects must understand that they correct one another, and that a limit, under the sun, shall curb them all. Each refuses to be God. Each tells the other that he or she is not God.

Our consciences are fallible. They are human instruments. They produce, at best, serviceable truths for our journey.

We do not choose to be born. We do not select our historical epoch, our parentage, the country of our birth, or the immediate circumstances of our upbringing. We do not, most of us, decide the time or circumstances of our death. But within these limitations, we do decide how we shall live: honorably or dishonorably, with purpose or adrift.

No matter how seemingly indifferent the universe may appear to our choices, they are ours to make. But it's scary to take one's destiny finally into one's own hands. Many folks turn down the option and all too willingly hand over their souls into another's keeping. Nonetheless, making choices remains at once the mortal peril and deathless splendor of our human lot.

I am often called upon to counsel individuals who feel trapped in painful impasses of indecision. Intellectually, even emotionally, they seem ready to execute a breakthrough and forge in a new direction. But they keep demurring: "I can't do it. I can't do it." To which I invariably say: "I believe you may not be ready to make the change. I even believe that perhaps you won't ever do it. But I will not agree that you *can't* do it. The *can't*s in your life are few, and this isn't one of them!"

We humans crave autonomy yet dread it. We fear, then avoid, making decisions. To determine our futures is at last to run the risk of falling or failing. These multiple fears are captured in the English phrase: "To take the plunge." Yet taking the plunge as card-carrying heretics is exactly what the religious course of Unitarian Universalism demands.

Sometimes we are stirred to imitate the courage of exemplary risk-takers. If we can just manage to take the first step, the rest will follow. Irish writer Frank O'Connor tells the story of how, as a boy, he and friends would make their way across the countryside, and when they came to an orchard wall that seemed too high and too difficult to permit their voyage to continue, they took off their hats and tossed them over the imposing wall. Then they had no choice but to follow them.

May we go and do likewise.

Freethinking

Dogmatism of any sort becomes blasphemous; it is the only real blasphemy.

—Phillip Hewitt

Muddlers in my opinion make the best liberals, and vice versa. Muddlers live somewhere between the certainty that is repeatedly wrong, and the uncertainty that leads to paralysis.

—Jack Mendelsohn

Unitarian Universalists harbor a liberal spirit more profound than intellectual agreement or theological sentiment. This essence cannot be squeezed into any fixed or final form, yet it is manifest in the disposition and directions of our faith. Our liberal attitude is evident when we embody affirmations that liberate rather than compromise or enslave others.

Being liberal has primarily to do with a frame of mind, an orientation to life and events. Therefore, what separates true liberals from false ones is not adherence to any particular organization or program, but rather our faithfulness to the unrestrained yet committed life.

At the same time, we must be vigilant against equating our free spirit with doctrinaire social, economic, or political liberalism. One of our seasoned ministers, Roger Greeley, advances our ancestry as freethinkers in his sermon "The History of Freethinkers":

> Unitarian Universalism is a place in which to grow as individuals in the direction of dreams long cherished by the progressive, sensitive, and creative people throughout the long pull of history. We are freethinkers. We are a free church for a changing world. We are not a liberal movement for liberal causes; let us leave those choices and courses of action to political parties and organizations specifically designed around those principles be they liberal or conservative. As freethinkers, our task is to keep the doors and windows open, to responsibly search forbidden paths and explore the unknown inhibited in that quest only by conscience and a concern for humanity.

I have chosen the term *freethinker* to be the pivotal modifier of the Unitarian Universalist way of religion, because I deem it a fresher and less corrupted reference than *liberal*. *Freethinking* also poses one of our central religious paradoxes: we are unencumbered pilgrims yet charged to engage in mental rigor. We dare not confuse freethinking with either free association or free feeling. There is nothing quite so pernicious as a free-swinging thinker with a lot of swing and precious little think, or what essayist Eric Hoffer described as "a homeless hitchhiker on the highways of the world thumbing a ride on any eternal cause that rolls by." On the contrary, freethinking is never a passive or facile process, but a stern discipline.

A wit once brooded that "the distinction between freedom and liberty is not accurately known, since naturalists have never been able to find a living specimen of either." Unitarian Universalists certainly aren't full-blown exemplars of free thought. Our lives remain riddled with subtle stiffness or bias, but our potentially saving grace is that our freethinking temper tends to keep us fluid and unshackled.

As fellow Unitarian Universalist Terry Sweetser puts it in "Free for What?":

> The word freedom comes from an ancient Norse root verb that means to become loving. Freedom is not properly a state of being then, but more accurately a choice for becoming. So, in our religion, freedom is about becoming, never about being.

At our truest, freethinkers keep expanding. We stay evergreen, avoiding psychosclerosis, the hardening of mind and spirit.

Pledging Our Troth

Now I don't think being agreed with is a fundamental human need, but I do think that being understood is.

—Jay Atkinson
"Lest One Good Custom Should Corrupt the World"

As a religious heritage bonded not by creed, confession, or common prayer but by covenant, Unitarian Universalists vow to stay at the table long enough to understand one another and mold a viable community. Ours is a fellowship united not by law but by loyalty, by faithfulness of vows rather than sameness of beliefs. We promise to hold and be held by one another. We pledge our troth or trust. Fidelity, internal discipline, and mutual responsibility are required in a covenantal faith in order to work out our differences together.

As a youngster I joined nearly everything. I managed to say no to membership campaigns so seldom that my yes was rendered nearly meaningless. In the second half of life, my attitude has altered drastically. I relate to, and certainly support, various enterprises, but I join few of them. Joining literally means "yoking oneself" in serious, abiding commitment, and I have become more discriminating. I prefer to travel my life's final laps lightly with but a handful of solid devotions. So, joining a Unitarian Universalist community is no idle matter; it has become one of my primary life-allegiances. Freethinkers generally identify with this reluctance to pledge our troth to people or institutions, but, once given, such commitments carry immense power in our lives.

In joining a local Unitarian Universalist congregation with a common history, shared liturgical practices, and binding ethical principles, we confess that we are not self-sufficient pilgrims. We admit that the warranty on our souls expires periodically, and we need an affinity group, through its patient prodding, to grant us an extension. We are not solitary figures, we are communitarians. Unitarian Universalism is a covenantal, partnered path, where independent wills dwell in the service of creating and sustaining an interdependent web of existence, not only with other humans but with the sacred circle of animals, plants, and deities that inhabit our universe.

The Reverend Gordon McKeeman reminds us that the derivation of the word *community*, although related to communion and communication, comes literally from the Latin *munio*, meaning "to arm." Therefore, with the prefix *com*, meaning "together," community happens wherever there is shared growth and security, a context of mutual succor and vigilance. Authentic Unitarian Universalist religious community consists of compassionate arms engaged in firm, fair, friendly wrestling matches rather than in bloodbaths of back-stabbing. Arms huddle together in times of sorrow and swing open in moments of rejoicing. Arms reach outward in justice-building and peace-making, not merely inward in narcissistic embrace. Arms offer forgiveness, the gift of a second chance. Arms defend against arrogance and shallowness, outside agitators or internal saboteurs.

Our Unitarian Universalist congregations constitute the joining of hearts and heads, souls and arms, and they depend on us stakeholders pledging our troth. We don't need to trust if we never seek permanent bonds while wandering this earth. But trust is necessary for those who choose the joint path of creative insecurity.

We are pilgrims who pledge our troth to uphold a beloved community of personal growth, social justice, and spiritual awakening—for better, for worse, forever. Troth is all we have to offer, but it should prove sufficient adhesive to bind us together for the length of our shared journey.

A sense of unshakable trust in the universe and humanity makes love achievable and death endurable.

Truthers

As a liberal traditionalist, I am also an existentialist, a relativist and a pragmatist. By existentialist I mean that truth must take its origin and be confirmed in personal experience. By relativist I see truth and human understanding of truth as inextricably related, so that the strongest truth claims must be made in a spirit of humility. And by pragmatist I look for the meaning of language in the live effects of ideas named, not in dictionaries.

—Alice Blair Wesley
"Things My Mother Taught Me: Gifts of Tradition"

Unitarian Universalists see ourselves as inveterate truth-seekers. However, there is more to this truth business than merely searching after it. According to John Hayward's *Existentialism and Religious Liberalism*, the painter Pablo Picasso, certainly ensconced in the free-thought tradition, passionately remarked:

> In my opinion, to search means nothing in painting. To find, is the thing. The one who finds something, no matter what it might be, at least

arouses our curiosity, if not our imagination. When I paint, my object is to show what I have found and not what I am looking for.

It becomes the fate of freethinkers to stake our lives on incomplete but satisfactory data, penultimate values if you will. We never enjoy total truth, only a sufficient supply of it, so we must live by successive approximations of the good, the loving, the beautiful.

In addition to seeking truth and finding truth, there is facing truth. An unremitting readiness to confront the facts can prove unsettling. There are truths we would rather ignore: truths about ourselves, our inherited assumptions, our backgrounds, our partners, even our cherished ideologies. But the mission of Unitarian Universalism remains to come together and, fortified with the nudges and embraces of companions, to stand tall and face whatever harsh truths existence delivers.

There is more. Speaking the truth is also an imperative for freethinkers. Telling the truth is more complicated than either lying or remaining silent. We belong to a legacy of prophets who assailed the social and theological orthodoxies of their day.

A *New Yorker* cartoon shows two people engaged in conversation at a social gathering. One says to the other: "That's where I part company with Unitarians, they have trouble telling lies!" Such a characterization of our faith isn't totally accurate, for we have exhibited our share of fibs and fabrications. Nonetheless, to become a people of integrity we aspire to approach a 90 percent truth-telling level. And when we do dare "to speak the truth in love," as the Bible urges, we do so not only for ourselves but also in honor of both our religious forebears and our spiritual descendants.

Unitarian Universalists seek after the truth, find some, face more, and tell as much as we can. Finally, whether we actualize our truths in daily life constitutes the litmus test of freethinking mystics with hands. Unitarian Universalist Buckminster Fuller said that "Truth is a verb . . . ," and the New Testament exhorts us, above all else, "to do the truth," not merely to chat about or fuss with it.

I think of the stirring witness of Albert Schweitzer: "My life—my argument." At the age of thirty, he stood at the peak of his promise: theologian, biblical scholar, professor at a great university, and lionized by the high and the mighty. Schweitzer gave it all up to serve in one of the most disadvantaged and difficult areas of the world at that time, equatorial Africa. There was sickness and sorrow enough for a thousand doctors. Schweitzer built a hospital with his own two hands. He begged for money to supply and staff it. When once he asked an educated, local friend to help him carry a heavy timber, the answer was, "I am an intellectual and don't carry timbers around!" To which Schweitzer replied: "You're lucky. I too wanted to become an intellectual, but I didn't make it!" He might better have said, "But I outgrew it!"

You and I belong to a reasonable faith, but we are scarcely a band of intellectuals. Rather, we are drafted to be truth-doers who lug, with our own hands, the necessary timbers to build a more just and joyful world.

Happy Low Sunday!

Perhaps we should realize that our need is not to "find something to believe"—but rather to discover what our lives indicate that we believe right now. This is the place to start.

—Edith Hunter

While planning a summer worship service on violence against women, I suddenly "got it." I realized that being a Unitarian Universalist activist meant doing the work of social justice guided by my theology, by my encounter with the divine and my understanding of spirit all the time, every day, in every circumstance. Once I got it, I couldn't go back. I was irrevocably committed to being a religious activist.

—Alison Cooper
"Confronting Evil:
An Activist Response to Violence"

In Unitarian Universalist congregations, the first Sunday after Easter is officially designated Low Sunday on the liturgical calendar—low in terms of both attendance and meaning. In contrast to Good Friday and Easter, things are quieter, slower, more daily. Laity often skip worship, and clergy are prone to go through the motions. But Low Sunday is a magnificent liturgical surprise, because it features the holy in the ordinary.

Our early church forebears felt that Low Sunday was connected to that passage in the Gospel of John where Jesus appeared after Easter to his disciples rather secretively and unexpectedly in a backroom to share private gestures of affection with his companions, especially "Doubting Thomas." The contrast with either Good Friday or Easter, both world-shaking spectaculars, is striking, yet it is precisely this unexpected time of life-giving touch in the unlikely corners of existence that manifests the sacred in the commonplace.

Low Sunday unveils the central tenet of our Unitarian Universalist faith: that religion at its fullest is discovered, not in the peaks or valleys of existence, but rather in the plains. God dwells in the details. As someone mused, "Look after the molehills and the mountains will look after themselves."

Hoping to obtain some lofty teaching, a novice once asked master Chao-chou: "I have just entered the fellowship and am anxious to learn the first principle of Zen. Will you please teach it to me?"

Chao-chou responded, "Have you eaten your supper?"

The novice replied, "I have."

"Then go wash your bowl!"

As freethinking mystics with hands we seek not dazzling states of ecstatic vision, nothing esoteric or abnormal, but the unclogging of our ears and the unblinding of our eyes that we might experience the mundane realities before us. Responsive religion turns on whether we ignore or address what Emerson called the "emphatic trifles" of everyday.

Tucked away amid lurid, grandiose news items in a metropolitan newspaper was this terse comment on the death of an actress: "She played minor parts exquisitely." Indeed, our lives are a mosaic of minor parts: dishwashing, writing letters, taking walks, answering phone calls, driving, breaking bread with family or friends, performing a hundred such pedestrian tasks. How we play out the prosaic roles in our daily drama reveals the depth and expanse of our character.

Good Friday relates the crucifixion of love. Easter proclaims that love breaks through tombs. Low Sunday reminds us that love is back on the job, and we should be on the lookout to be touched, even amidst our doubting.

Room for Everyone

There is room on our path for any person who seeks a more complete understanding of what is true and good in life. The answers can't be found if you ask only men. They can't be found if you ask only Christians. They can't be found if you ask only gay people. They can't be found if you ask just yourself. The answers come from listening to people of great diversity and weaving their small truths into a larger tapestry of Meaning.

—David Blanchard
Unitarian Universalist Lesbian Gay Caucus Newsletter

What I know about being inclusive—crossing from culture to culture, learning the language of diversity—is that it's the work of a lifetime. It's hard to accept people who are not like you. . . . Nothing that Unitarian Universalists need to do is more important than making justice real—here, where we are. Hard as diversity is, it is our most important task.

—Rosemary Bray McNatt
"It's Hard Work"
Been in the Storm So Long

All of us have felt strange in certain settings, have been treated as strangers at one time or another, have suffered the anguish of an estranged relationship. Consequently, we can identify with being welcomed inside life's house of hospitality rather than standing outside in the cold. "Hospitality to strangers is greater than reverence for the name of God," says the Hebrew proverb, and the New Testament affirms the same message when it declares: "I was a stranger and you took me in." Our Unitarian Universalist version of unconditional welcome is stated by John Hays Nichols in his sermon "Can Two Walk Together?":

> We believe that if there is a loving God, this God will save all souls. If, in some other realm, there is a great clubhouse of souls, everybody's getting in. Catholics, Protestants, Jews, Muslims, agnostics, atheists: everybody's getting in.

We come into this world solitary. We depart the same way. We're meant to spend life's interval bridging incalculable gulfs—fostering companionships and building communities. Authentic religious community mandates inclusion of those individuals different from ourselves who display strange customs or foreign views. Moreover, we are summoned not merely to endure but to enjoy these differences. Otherwise, our community unwittingly devolves into a cozy club or an insular coalition.

No other creature appears to cast aside territorial and familial definitions and welcome the wanderer with words like these: "You are among your family," a traditional greeting to the guest among the Bedouin. There is the offer of a bath, a meal, and shelter to the stranger, gifts that correspond to the fundamental needs of one who travels as well as to the modest resources of one who dwells.

The minimum questions that determine whether or not a group of people is welcoming are "Who is being left out?" and "Would someone notice if I didn't show up?" The inclusive religious community doesn't stop there. It offers more than bath and bed; it extends the opportunity to co-create a redemptive community through dialogue and ceremony, education and good works.

Contemporary African American poet June Jordan cuts to the quick by asserting: "My hope is that our lives will declare this meeting open." But our culture doesn't have a very good track record with diversity. Most of our human meetings, including those of our own freethinking faith, tend in practice to be elitist and exclusionary. We merely tolerate strangers, squinting at them through the distorted lens of prejudice and fear. While tolerating differences of theology, orientation, and race in theory, we gravitate by habit toward homogeneity of lifestyle, social behavior, and rituals. Others all too quickly become outsiders, even opponents. Yet it is our prophetic imperative to keep our meetings open, to stay at the table. Though frail and flawed, Unitarian Universalists continue to struggle to build a house of hospitality.

In matters of diversity, we have grown increasingly more comfortable with the term *acceptance* than *tolerance*, and now *inclusion* seems the most precise word. But clearly tolerance, acceptance, and inclusion inhabit the same family of meaning. For us *PC* doesn't refer to "political correctness" but instead to our marred yet persistent efforts to be personally compassionate, prophetically courageous, and pluralistically celebrative.

The call to tolerance can evoke another demon. Counterfeit acceptance degenerates into *anythingarianism* (Jonathan Swift's term) when intolerable behaviors and conditions, whether in society or our local churches, are permissible, even justified. In the name of so-called tolerance we put up with despicable human conduct and pervasive human misery. We lapse into lassitude. Tolerance becomes a disguise for indifference!

But let us be neither lulled nor fooled. We can't engender justice without also being intolerant of injustice, we can't dignify freedom without eradicating slavery, we can't applaud beauty if we are rationalizing ugliness. The Unitarian Universalist heritage has been filled with troublemakers who were absolutely intolerant ("creatively maladjusted," to use Martin Luther King Jr.'s phrase) of anything that was injurious to the body and spirit of their fellow creatures.

With telling frequency, especially in ancient languages, *host* and *guest* are the same word. We humans recognize both roles. Ultimately, we are all strangers and welcomers at the gate, life members in the fellowship of wanderers, huddling close and taking our turns against the wind. Our churches become caves in which to give and receive shelter, practicing the ancient, holy rite of hospitality.

Faithful to Beauty
and the Humiliated

Beauty is not down another road. It is a response each of us must make for ourselves; must, or Satan has won and humankind is condemned to ugliness. Beauty is not in the eye, or even in the heart, of the beholder. It is in our entire selves; our nerves and muscles, our histories and minor choices.

—R. C. A. Moore
Words for the Wind

In the mix of beauty and injustice that marks any religious tradition, we must judge what gives life and what oppresses. We must take our place as appraisers and stewards of religious value.

—Rebecca Parker
"After the Apocalypse"
The Transient and Permanent in Liberal Religion

There is an ancient Persian adage that says if you have two pennies, spend one on a loaf of bread and share it with the hungry, and with the other buy a flower and revel in its magnificence. As freethinking mystics with hands Unitarian Universalists turn our souls outward in acts of mercy and inward through communion with art and nature.

I am blessed to have married into a family that appreciates beauty at the very core of their lives. It doesn't dwell in their eyes, even their hearts alone, but permeates their nerves and muscles, histories and choices. They create beauty wherever they settle. Without beauty their lives would, by their own admission, be utterly impoverished.

Occasionally, I feel like the student living in my dorm at college who would play Mozart's *Eine Kleine Nachtmusik* over and over. One day I asked him, "You know, I have the impression that when you really need inspiration, you play Mozart's *Eine Kleine Nachtmusik*." "Yes, I do," he replied. "Why?" I asked. "Well," he said, "when I hear that piece of music, I say to myself, I may never be able to become the incredible scholar I'd like to be, but at least I belong to a race of human beings who produced a Mozart who wrote *Eine Kleine Nachtmusik*. And that recognition keeps me going forward!"

Beauty is always a good in and of itself, quite apart from any utilitarian or social value it might possess. We human beings are entitled to bask in a sunset, dance to a Viennese waltz, be enthralled by a watercolor sketch—all without any particular objective in mind. In truth, religion begins at the level of myth, ritual, and art rather than with concepts or theologies.

Unitarian Universalism perceives beauty not only as a quality that charms the senses, but also as a virtue that ennobles the soul. Remember, we hold two pennies in our hands: one for flowers, the other for bread. Consequently, Unitarian Universalists don't have the luxury of basking in beauty without leading lives of goodness as well, or conversely, giving ourselves sacrificially to the oppressed while ignoring the grandeur of existence. In *Lyrical and Critical Essays*, the French existentialist Albert Camus put it well: "There is beauty and there are the humiliated. Whatever difficulties the enterprise may present, I would like never to be unfaithful either to the one or the other."

Of course, there will always be those among us who resonate especially to music, art, dance, and the wonders of nature, while others find supreme meanings through social justice. These two groups often quarrel over priorities in the execution of local parish business, sometimes to the point that one questions whether the other really belongs in the Unitarian Universalist fold. Well, both do.

We are called to be ambidextrous, both sharers of beauty and builders of justice. Playing these two orientations against one another is bad doctrine and poor politics. Our faith is spacious enough to encompass an astounding array of opinions and behaviors. Fellow Unitarian Universalists who grate on our nerves are frequently the very people who stretch our horizons the most.

Harry Scholefield, who always juggled the challenges of personal growth, social witness, and spiritual integrity in a balanced Unitarian Universalist ministry, was once pressed: "Harry, how do you produce an effective social action program?" His response was telling: "To start with, you have a good music program!" Yes. And the opposite holds as well. If we want to provide a vital fine-art experience in our local congregations, then we had better foster strong social witness as well.

Why? Because if we deliver our souls to the artistic side of our faith, we will undoubtedly be inspired to be vigorous carriers of social justice. And conversely, if we labor unstintingly in the vineyards as compassionate persons, we will wear thin without the refreshment provided by the beautiful.

As freethinking mystics with hands, Unitarian Universalists must constantly balance principles like freedom and responsibility, doubt and belief, sorrow and joy, beauty and justice. To lead saved lives we must become whole persons who pursue both the restoration of our spirits through beauty and the reformation of our society through service.

We are all wanderers passing through the universe for but a brief spell. Assuredly, there is no finer way to spend our earthly stint than by singing and serving, serving and singing, in rhythmic fashion, all the way to the grave.

Mystics

Our scientists are not solving mysteries, they are making discoveries. Nor is mystery the same as magic. . . . Mystery is an awareness. It is the wonder at the simple holiness of life itself. Mystery leads us to stand in awe of the fact that we do exist, that the world in all its beauty *is*.

—Joyce Smith
"The Four M's of Religion"

Often with all our openness and freespiritedness on the mountain of wisdom, we don't climb high enough. Religion is the heart soaring to heights the head will never know. Climb at least to the timberline, but what a pity if we fail to climb to the summit and experience the presence of something from everlasting to everlasting.

—Waldemar Argow

Whereas the rationalist strain in our Unitarian Universalist heritage is well documented, our mystical inclinations lie concealed. We have been satirized as a demystified religion suffering from an "ecstasy deficit." Even while applauding the prodigious contributions of Unitarian transcendentalists such as Ralph Waldo Emerson and Margaret Fuller, we often fail to acknowledge their pervasive mystical bent. Yet the truth remains as expressed by President Louis Cornish of the American Unitarian Association in 1937: "We belong among the mystics." We need to claim, then internalize, the portion of our heritage that experiences the universe numinously.

Contemporary Unitarian Universalist Mark Belletini heartily underlines this temperament in *What Unitarian Universalists Believe*:

> Mysticism marks our movement as much as our more famous rationalism and has always done so. By mysticism I do not mean privileged revelation or occultism, though the word is sometimes, sadly, used that way. . . . Any crisp definition of mysticism would belie the truth. In seeking provisionally to define "mysticism," I need to find phrasing strong enough to bear much richness yet which rings clear as a bell. And so I come to the elegant words of our shared Principles: "[Mysticism signifies the] direct experience of that transcending mystery and wonder, affirmed in all cultures, which moves us to a renewal of the spirit." And this mysticism of the direct experience is as much

a source of our splendid Christianities, Theisms, and Humanisms as is our reasoned critique.

Rationalism without a sense of mystery grows sterile, and mysticism untempered by reason falls prey to credulity. Unitarian Universalists are freethinking mystics. As bona fide mystics, the substance of our faith points to an ineffable yet undeniable connection with sacrality, both mysterious and sustaining. Unitarian Universalist mystics proclaim two main convictions: our lives are embraced by a mystery that is gracious and trustworthy, and our human fulfillment lies in surrendering to it.

Unitarian Universalism comes to full fruition when we freethinking mystics give birth to rituals of praise and deeds of mercy, or as the Shaker tradition suggests: "Hearts to God, hands to work." Our reasonable, liberating visions of holiness are restless until incarnated.

Where We Are Planted

We need to experience Earth's forgiveness, Earth's renewal, Earth's abundant graciousness. I used to think we need to save the Earth. Now I think maybe it is Earth that is saving us.

—Carol Hepokoski
"Ecofeminism: Healing the Earth and Ourselves"

My roots run deep in the soil of California. I am animated by a visceral passion for the ocean, the redwoods, and the desert, and while I have weathered countless earthquakes over the years, I feel profound respect, not terror, in the face of these unpredictable convulsions. Most naturalists accent the lush greens and deep blues of California's scenery; I prefer the sensuous, golden-brown tones of our undulating hills. I am proud that my ancestors go back several generations in Southern California, with my grandmother Clorinda Ramirez riding on one of the first Rose Parade floats.

Our respect, however, needs to be not only for the earth we all inhabit, but also for our individual bodies. May we employ to the fullest the one body we have received—a good though imperfect gift. May we make sure that our body is well nourished rather than defiled, regardless of the length of our earthly trek. I can think of no better prayer to repeat daily with respect to our bodies than the familiar Serenity Prayer: "God, grant me the courage to change the things I can (about my body), the serenity to accept the things I cannot change (about my body), and the wisdom to know the difference."

Our bodies will at length return to the earth—we go from dust to dust. That being true, it is critical to affirm not only our carnal pleasures but also the burdens to which our flesh is heir. May we never lust after another's embodiment or homeland or profession.

Wherever we are planted is precisely where we are to manifest ourselves as freethinking mystics with hands. Spirituality and geography are braided together. We won't discover *who* we really are without submitting fully to *where* we are. There is our tilling ground, our battleground, our growing ground.

Nothing Human Is Alien to Me

Evil is related to emptiness. It fills a void.
Where good is not consciously active and
diligent, evil enters. . . . Let us accept our
responsibility with more grace than guilt.
Thinking collectively, let our liberal religious
community remember that we are a part of
the whole, and if the whole is wounded, we
are wounded as well.

—Elizabeth Ellis-Hagler
"Ministering to the Wounded"

Tonight I repent of my smugness. Tonight I
acknowledge that I speak to you all as a recovering sexist among recovering sexists who share
membership in a religious institution which
still has far to go before resting on any laurels.
I speak in the spirit of the Polish Unitarians of
the mid-seventeenth century who wrote in a
new preface to their catechism: "We do not
think that we ought to be ashamed if in some
respect our church improves."

—Katharine Winthrop
"A Response to the Sophia Fahs Lecture
Presented by Carter Heyward"

Unitarian Universalism, in its 400-plus-year history, has claimed that humans begin in good shape with the prospect of getting better. We have been perennially soft on sin and evasive with evil. We have observed that people behave badly, that they do downright wicked things, but our focus has been on the improvability, even perfectibility, of humankind. "Onward and upward forever" has been our essential refrain.

The twentieth century has been sobering to romantic liberals. Progress, it turned out, was not automatic. The impulse to lie, to hurt, to kill has not been civilized out of us. Inexplicable travail and intractable evil come with the territory of being alive and human. You know the story of the farmer who lay down in his barn and cried out, "How long, O God, am I going to suffer from this famine?" A voice from beyond responded, "Seven years." The farmer then asked, "And what's going to happen, O God, after seven years?" The voice from beyond answered, "You'll get used to it!" Evil is here to stay.

Our theological assessment of human nature has been considerably chastened, and we are forced by the facts to live with heightened unease, but as the Reverend Alma Crawford reminds us: "Discomfort, like prayer, fasting, and yoga, can become a spiritual discipline." Our cheerful band of religious liberals must now practice our faith in light of human behavior that is incurably ambiguous, complex, and varied. Everyone, including ourselves, is capable of both deep caring and destructive aggression, moments of the sublime and the bestial. All our solid thinking, mystical consciousness, and benevolent hands can diminish but never fully dislodge evil.

The 1985 UUA Principles place matters in proper perspective. On the one hand, "we are challenged to confront powers and structures of evil with justice, compassion, and the transforming power of love," indicating our capacity as carriers of kindness to make a considerable dent in the powers of evil. On the other hand, we are warned "against idolatries of the mind and spirit." Clearly, one of the insidious idols of an activist, do-good religion such as ours is the cockiness of believing we can conquer the principalities of evil merely through force of mind or spirit. Therefore, Unitarian Universalists must walk the fine line between paralyzing apathy and overweening confidence.

The mandatory first step in addressing evil is to acknowledge our own complicity in it. Before fighting it in the outside world, we must recognize palpable evil in our picayune malices and stealthy deceits, our unworthy fears and hurtful hostilities displayed both privately and publicly.

In a *Peanuts* comic strip, Charlie Brown is eating a peanut butter and jelly sandwich. He looks admiringly at his hands and says:

> Hands are fascinating things. I like my hands. . . . I think I have nice hands. My hands

seem to have a lot of character. These are hands that may someday accomplish great things. These are hands that may someday do marvelous works. They may build mighty bridges or heal the sick, or hit home runs, or write soul-stirring novels. These are hands that may someday change the course of destiny!

Lucy looks down at Charlie's hands and says: "They've got jelly on them!" Lucy's comment, albeit insensitive, is right on target.

Not everything that is faced can be changed, but nothing can be changed until it is faced. Hence, we start by recognizing that our own hands are covered with jelly. And they always will be. But they are all we have. They are who we are. Messy to be sure, we keep using our hands in acts of justice and kindness that life might be less evil.

Doubting Believers

The theology of doubt is the underlying theology of Unitarian Universalism. . . . It's a theology which keeps us from self-righteousness, but not action. . . . So let's cherish our doubts. They not only lead to larger truth, but they make us wise, keep us humble, and allow us to live together in love.

—Christine Robinson
"Cherish Your Doubts"

Unitarian Universalists may not be born skeptics, but sooner or later we develop a passion for the art of creative doubt. We are not comfortable in being intellectually stodgy and spiritually quiescent. We question because we are willing to grow. Desiring a supportive clan in which to expand our horizons, we end up in the Unitarian Universalist fold.

However, we soon realize that doubt by itself isn't enough. We choose to live *with* doubt but not *by* doubt. We live beyond reason and despite doubt; we live by faith. Doubt alone leads to despair, in which we slide from healthy skepticism into a debilitating cynicism that negates the spirit of life.

Much of my life is grounded in faith. My wife and I share multiple evidences of our love as well as vexatious doubts. But the foundation of our love rests upon faith in our good will, our stable commitment, our abiding intimacy.

Faith is integral to my communion with self, neighbor, nature, and God. In all these covenants, I proceed deliberately but confidently, despite partial knowledge and flawed vision.

To be mature, doubting believers we seek comrades who will keep us awake and on course. A religious community is where our faith can be celebrated, stretched, and refined. It is where we can share the burdens of our doubts and our temptations to despondency. It is where our faith can be spurred to extend outward to serve the larger world. A Midrash reinforces the need to share such religious community:

> God said to Moses: "You doubted me, but I forgive you that doubt. You doubted your own powers as a leader, and I forgive you that also. But you lost faith in this people and doubted the divine possibilities of human nature. That I cannot forgive. That loss of faith makes it impossible for you to enter the Promised Land.

It is foolhardy either to doubt or to believe all by oneself!

Moving from Gratitude to Compassion

> Ours is a church of moral work—not because we think morality is a sufficient religion, but because we know no better way of showing our gratitude to God, and our confidence in one another.
>
> —Wallace Robbins
> "A Liberal Church"
> *Hymns for the Celebration of Life*

We are the blessed beneficiaries of this tumultuous, wonder-filled existence, a gracious gift beyond either our deserving or earning, and our holiest response from morn to night is to shout "thank you god for most this amazing day . . . " (e. e. cummings). Living in a state of thankfulness, having our cups full, we naturally overflow. For the graced or grateful person there is simply no other way to respond to unmerited love than to exude compassion all the way to the grave, and count not the cost. We have been known to serve others out of sympathy or duty, even from fear or guilt, but authentic compassion is born out of gratitude.

Compassion literally refers to expressing profound feeling or sentiment with another: to passion, as it were, beside other life. Compassion is marked by a tenacious, limber tenderheartedness. It denotes the agility to assist others without becoming mired in their crisis.

Religious educator Elizabeth Strong relates the story of a little girl sent by her mother on an errand. When she finally returned, the mother asked what took her so long. A friend had broken his bicycle, and she had stopped to help. "But," her mother said, "you don't know anything about fixing bicycles." "I know," she said. "I stopped to help him cry!" Without fail, the call to be compassionate is not to remedy a problem but to place ourselves alongside hurting individuals, "weeping with those who weep," as the biblical phrase goes. Our inner human soil must be watered with tears— kept moist, soft.

There is more to compassion than solely comforting the mournful or rejoicing with celebrants. Constructive defiance or righteous rage qualifies as well. Compassionate people care enough to confront others with negative feelings. Anger, rather than hostility, arrives as a charitable gift.

There is a lovely expression, "to be moved with compassion," in the Gospels. The Greek verb, *splangchnizomai*, reveals the gutsy power entailed in "being moved with compassion," for *splangchna* are the entrails of the human body, designating precisely where our most intense emotions, ranging from gladness to fury, reside.

Another reminder about compassion: The word can be read as *com-patience*, because the words *passion* and *patience* both find their roots in the same Latin word *pati*. So it is prudent to remember that compassion is a virtue demonstrated largely by the plodders and perseverers among us rather than the flashy and impulsive. Patience reminds religious wayfarers to "hasten slowly," traveling with steady gaze and sure foot on the sacred path—bearing pain, delight, and anger alongside our sisters and brothers. "Alongside" is the precise word, since compassionate action is not done *for* others so much as *with* others. It is even *for* ourselves in a profound sense, because being compassionate helps fulfill our very humanity.

Compassion, the genuine article, is shown first toward ourselves and our family, then to animals and other weaker, marginalized creatures, and finally spreads abroad into the greater community, enfolding all who cross our trail. The sad fact is that Unitarian Universalists, equipped with an impassioned conscience, are often more demonstrative in our social outreach to outsiders in need than we are in caring for the hurting members of our own families and congregations.

However, in all ways and places, compassionate people are enjoined to "love thy neighbor *as* thyself." There is an implied equal sign in that biblical phrase, for if we don't love ourselves, then we have little of worth and substance to offer our neighbor. The indisputable truth is that compassion is indivisible.

The Unitarian Universalist cadence is compelling: to awake with gratitude on our lips for the unmerited gift of yet another day of living, then to cascade with compassion.

With Hands

May the work of our hands match the mode
of their making. Hand-clasp bringing friend-
liness. Hand-soothe bringing help and healing. . . . Hands that bring shelter and sanctuary.
Hands of applause for work well done and
words well taken. All hands in time of trouble!
May the work and touch of our hands be as
prayer in the temples of the world. May the
guilt of our hands be expunged not by wring-
ing them in despair, but by setting them to
the plough.

—Leonard Mason
Bold Antiphony

In our religious communities we celebrate
touching: hands share life when they meet
another's. Hands tell us we are valuable, we
are loved, we are welcome, and we are not
alone. How sensitively we handle inanimate
objects. Let us handle one another with simi-
lar care. Please touch. In praise of hands and
hearts, please touch.

—Carolyn Owen-Towle
"In Praise of Hands"

The human hand is a wondrous marvel. It sets us apart from the rest of the animal population by its ability not only to grasp but to extend. Designed for gripping and touching, each hand has up to 1,300 nerve endings per square inch. Sensations of touch are even more complex than sight or hearing because most of them are mixtures of several stimuli. Touch is the first sense to ignite and frequently the final one to fade. Long after our eyes or ears fail us, our hands stretch forth to define our world. Therefore, in describing the close of our earthly sojourn, we often talk simply about "losing touch."

Our hands, at their noblest, are lifted in praise, shaken in friendship, spread in loving embrace, folded in prayer, aroused to clapping, thrust in resistance, unfurled to welcome the alien and enfold the needy. Lest we over-romanticize, our hands have also been known to spank, slap, assault, to deliver harm rather than to heal. Tomas Firle, member of a "Stopping Gender Violence" working group, has created a liturgy based on using our hands in service of peaceful choices. He closes with these words:

> As I look at my hands now, I invite you to look at yours. Yes, my hands have hit and hurt. But I have a choice: no more! My hands are beautiful! They express my creativity, they caress. I ask you now to meditate on a pledge that I have made and invite you to make as well:

My hands were not made or meant for hitting. My hands shall not hit or hurt another person. My hands are made to create, to caress! And that shall be the expression of myself.

Brother Firle's gender-healing work reminds me of the story of the Buddha that Sheldon Kopp recounts. It illustrates our religious duty to raise one hand against fear, followed by extending the other in compassion.

Determined to destroy the Buddha, a treacherous demon unleashed an elephant, which charged drunkenly at the Buddha. Just as the furious beast was about to trample him, the Buddha raised his right hand with fingers held close together and open palm facing the oncoming animal. This fearless gesture stopped the elephant in its tracks and completely subdued the dangerous creature.

Once having faced the terrible threat of annihilation, the compassionate Buddha extended his other hand with its palm up, as if cupping the gift of an open heart. This charitable gesture of forgiveness restored the elephant's natural tranquillity. And so proceeds our human passage: hands thrust in resistance *and* hands offered in conciliation.

Hands carry even more associations to them. Think of those who have arthritic or deformed hands. Think of hands underappreciated, abused, or undeveloped in their use because their possessors were told they were unworthy. Think of hands of applause, the healing hand of argument, calloused hands, the slayer's hands, the craftsperson's hands, and remember those hands that were pierced with nails for all to view the agony. And just think, if it weren't for her hands, Helen Keller might have been eternally closeted in darkness and silence.

Ponder the words, not all positive, that include the root word *hand*: handout, hand-me-down, on the other hand, openhanded, underhanded, handshake, hand-in-glove, unhand me, glad-hander, handbook, the laying on of hands.

Reflect upon realities that remain truly out of your hands, then let them go. Conversely, entertain possibilities that nestle in your grasp, then handle them with exceeding care.

We come into existence with our fists clenched as babies, but when we arrive at death's door our hands are open. During the intervening lifetime, we are summoned to progressively unclench our fists and open our hands in love and concern toward all who crisscross our path.

The Enduring Center of Unitarian Universalism

> We need to learn the art of holding on easily.
> Much is going to be taken away, slip away, or
> be destroyed. We can let go. What holds on
> to us is far more important.
>
> —John Taylor
> *Notes on an Unhurried Journey*

Unitarian Universalism designates my faith and my
institutional allegiance. While this covenantal identity
is firm, my theological convictions are varied and shift-
ing. Let's see. I am a mystical humanist with naturalistic leanings and receptivity to disclosures of the divine.
I meander comfortably amid the Judeo-Christian mo-
tifs and stories of my heritage. My religious vision is
tempered by existentialism, grounded in earth-centered
spiritualities, aligned with the wisdoms of Asian tradition, especially Taoism, and bathed in trustful agnosticism. In short, as Walt Whitman mused, "Do I
contradict myself? Yes, I contain multitudes."

At a conference, when given fifteen minutes to define our enduring Unitarian Universalist center in
thirty words or less, I wrote: "Everyone is worthy and
welcome to worship, grow, and serve as they choose in

our religious community, which is held in the universal embrace of eternal love." What would you say?

Here's a longer rendition.

First, Unitarianism. Central to the very word and tradition is the conviction that every *unit* of existence—animal, plant, or human—is sacred and to be treated as such. Everyone is welcome at our intergenerational table regardless of color or belief, gender or political view, orientation or capacity, class or age. No one is excluded. Every unit is prized.

Unitarianism also represents the *unity* of God, the claim that we are partners in an interdependent web of existence, that despite the welter of life forces buzzing throughout creation, there abides an indisputable oneness at the heart of reality. Creation is a *uni*-verse not a multi-verse. We did not create the ecosystem; our obligation is to live according to its inherent guidelines, honoring its unity as biological fact and source of religious aspiration.

In sum, at the center of my Unitarian faith is an unyielding confidence that every person is *unique* and valued and that ultimate reality is *unified*.

My Universalist side claims love as central. Universalism trusts that all of us are *held* in the arms of universal love, no matter what we have done or not done. *Held* is the operative term. This day, and throughout one's entire life, the full-blown cosmos rests in the grasp of a loving power. Such is the overruling Universalist affirmation.

Universalists are concerned about tomorrow and work ceaselessly to make society more beautiful and just, but we relinquish the final results. There is a rabbinical tale to the effect that theology means brooding over what God is worrying about when God arises in the morning. Well, if anything, God stews about repairing creation's brokenness. If that's true, then that's precisely what we humans ought to be worrying about too, concerned enough to do our share of the mending. But we should not be so worried that we cannot let go of our efforts and outcomes, surrendering them back to the mystery from whence we came. For what ultimately holds us, no matter what we have accomplished or failed to accomplish on earth, is a loving God.

We spend our entire lives not *repaying*, which we can't possibly do, but rather *responding* to this infinite spirit of love. Loved, we love in return. The Reverend Tracey Robinson-Harris relates the story of a five-year-old boy who, in the middle of a long and frightening night, wakes up in tears. He was staying with his grandfather as his parents tried to put the pieces of their lives back together again. He did not know what would happen to them or to himself.

When the boy awoke, he called out, "Grandpa, I'm scared." "It's all right," said Grandpa. "I'm here, I'm here." And indeed he was, sleeping in the other bed in the same room, right there, asleep yet alert, listening for his grandson's cry. The boy heard the reassuring words, "I'm here," yet, still crying, he said: "I know, Grandpa, but is your face turned toward me?"

That's the quintessential Universalist query: Is our face really turned toward the loved one, the stranger, even the enemy? Do we truly see others as worthy human beings? Being held in the grip of God's love, Universalism bids us to reciprocate love's favor, to turn fully toward the other, to look our sister and brother squarely in the face, with a steady, appreciative gaze.

We live in a world where people are damned in the name of religion because their views are different, are verbally and physically attacked because either the hue of their skin or the manner of their loving is different. Those of us who are held fast in the grasp of a loving faith must demonstrate an alternative way of being—the Universalist way of unqualified acceptance.

What is the enduring center of my Unitarian Universalist faith? Mine is a resolute belief in the unity of reality and the conviction that love is the undergirding principle of that reality; most important, I, as one human creature, am called upon during my earthly stay to treat our universe as unified and to add my ounces of love to the mix.

God-Fearing Humanists

The humanist and the theist live in me, each sometimes puzzled by the presence of the other, but willing to keep talking. So may it continue.

—Frances West
"When Theists and Humanists Sound Different
and Mean the Same Thing"

There is no reason to pitch out humanism now that there is a desire for more spirituality. No parts of our Living Tradition negate or cancel out the others. And I pray (yes, I pray!) that I will not be "drummed out" of humanism because I also call myself a liberal Christian (a follower of the teachings of Jesus), a Zen Buddhist (a believer in the power of presence and paradox) and a pagan (a lover of earthly and natural delights). My style of Unitarian Universalism values theological language, ritual and worship that speaks to the heart and soul as well as to the mind and ain't I a humanist?

—Melanie Morel Sullivan
"Ain't I a Humanist?"

Mystical humanism is perhaps the most intractable paradox we Unitarian Universalists have ridden throughout our history. Some do it side-saddle, tentatively, others with both hands to the reins and galloping full-bore ahead. Regardless, it provides a spirited jaunt!

Unitarian Universalists are *humanists* in the uncompromising sense that, in the last analysis, we define ourselves in terms of human duties, perceptions, and yearnings. We simply do not possess a god's-eye view of reality. Hence, it is our human imperative to live with as much humaneness, humility, and humor as conceivable. Whereas we need bountiful confidence as earthlings, we avoid brashness and arrogance, since we are mere mortals, neither angels nor deities.

As freethinking mystics, we try to place ourselves in proper perspective, recognizing our gifts and wounds, our capabilities and poverties. Humans are not the measure of all things but significant contributors. As our seventh principle reminds us, we have "respect for the interdependent web of all existence of which we are a part." We are neither irrelevant nor central, but rather an integral *part*!

Unitarian Universalists are, both historically and philosophically, a *God-fearing* bunch of humanists to be sure—not in the sense that we are terrified by or grovel before deity, but because we fully respect the creative, transforming power that brought us into being, nourishes us along the way, and refuses to relinquish its loving hold on us.

Indisputably, to become a robust, attractive faith for the twenty-first century, we must surpass arid rationalism and mindless mysticism. We will have to transcend the humanist-theist controversy and produce a fresh integration, something like what Unitarian minister Lester Mondale called "the middle realm of the spirit," permitting the savvy of each perspective to seep into our spiritual constitution. We need to endorse the viewpoint of John Haynes Holmes who found "no contradiction between humanism and theism but rather discovered in the one the fulfillment and completion of the other."

In truth, Unitarian Universalism comprises a breed today not unlike those Unitarian leaders, more than fifty years ago, who composed the Humanist Manifesto while still acknowledging boundless appreciation of divine mystery. In effect, most signers were naturalistic mystics positing that: "We humans are co-partners with great Nature which has produced us."

I like to characterize Unitarian Universalists as practicing atheists, agnostics, and affirmatists, balancing the three in fruitful tension. We are *atheists* because there are certain deities that we consider degrading, even downright dangerous, which, when promoted by us humans, have generated enormous terror, guilt, and bigotry across the years.

Humanism invites us to reject provincial and petty gods who suspend the laws of nature, play favorites among the races or nations of this globe, and whose wills are supposedly responsible for premature deaths and cosmic catastrophes. Alan Watts has a marvelous phrase for this torching of straw gods. He calls it "atheism in the name of God."

We are *agnostic* in that we Unitarian Universalists don't pretend, or even desire, to claim inside information about divine mystery. We are content to remain trustful unknowers. Humanism offers another staunch warning to those "hunting the divine fox": that none of our words are able to bring us closer to the presence of God. All discourse about God is inevitably analogical, drenched in human metaphor. Theology must never claim too much for itself. It points toward only the faintest echo of ultimate reality.

There is also the matter of God traveling incognito, arriving in unexpected places under pseudonyms, confronting us in disquieting fashion, such as when Isaiah believed that the Eternal was working through the pagan Assyrians to arouse the Israelites from their disobedience. All these unpredictable appearances of divinity should keep us humble and edgy.

Finally, we are *affirmatists* in that there are various names and faces of the divine that we consider meaningful, such as creator, sustainer, transformer, and judge. Unitarian Universalists are charged to find personally tailored ways of cultivating closer ties with divine mystery. We may open our hearts to deeper communion with God through song or dance, meditation or prayer, words or silence. As Emerson wrote:

"Let us be silent, that we may hear the whispers of the Gods."

But more than discussing the mystery of God or experiencing the presence of God within our souls, we are urged to love God through our acts of kindness and justice, thereby infusing ourselves with the eternal Spirit. Love is an activity more than a commodity, and we love God chiefly not by study, or even prayer, but by loving the universe and all its inhabitants with full mind and heart and might. Gandhi, a mystical activist, reported that he never found God in person but only in action.

Think of the tree as one primary image of the cosmos as an organic system of meanings. It consists of a huge canopy of branches above, an unseen but vast system of roots below, and a trunk linking and separating these two complex networks. A tree has the remarkable ability to grow both up and down, at the same time. As God-fearing humanists, and all other self-ascribed combinations on the theological continuum, we are challenged to grow in both directions, simultaneously receiving sustenance from heaven *and* earth.

Open, Not Empty, Minded

Let me keep the doors of my mind open for the possible knock of some vagrant truth. Let me swing wide the shuttered windows of my heart that perchance some winged messenger of love light upon my sill.

—Clinton Lee Scott
Promise of Spring

Gertrude Stein once said: "It is not what Paris gives you; it is what she does not take away," a remark intensely true of Unitarian Universalism as well. We can't give our members everything. We won't possibly meet one's grandest desires nor should we even try. Nonetheless, when we are faithful to our calling as freethinking mystics, we can promise an open setting in which all of us can stretch our minds and buttress our spirits. Unitarian Universalists will not be stripped of their integrity.

The Unitarian Universalist faith features neither the certain mind nor the empty mind. Instead, it fosters an open mind that can confront a novel proposal, handle an old wound, explore uncharted territory. We have forged a community where the air is fresh and flowing freely. We tend to resemble the concluding remark of Phyllis McGinley in her poem "The Mind Open at Both Ends": "I was born to shiver in the draft of an open mind."

Unitarian Universalists come by our religious values democratically. The principles we hold are not *revealed* to us so much as *experienced* by us. We freely examine every idea that comes down the pike, keeping for tenets of faith only those that prove truthful to ourselves and loving of others.

Parish minister Burdette Backus drew a critical distinction when he penned:

> We sometimes hear it said by some of our own members that you can believe whatever you please. Actually we are confronted with a paradox; we are not free to believe what we please, we are free to believe what we *must*!

There are tantalizing fantasies Unitarian Universalists are tempted to believe, but our minds won't let us. We live wholeheartedly within this single, real world and affirm only what our minds, after measured reflection, authorize us to affirm!

In short, to be a Unitarian Universalist requires one to shun intellectual laziness and spiritual shoddiness. We cannot rest easy with the faith we inherited. We must grow our own, revising it continually during our lifetime. We are blessed (perhaps cursed) with a faith as large as the universe, as diverse as human nature, and as complex as it is simple.

The open mind is a clogged mind if it never changes. Whenever we "arrive" in our spiritual quest, we ossify and turn, like Lot's wife, into useless pillars of salt. During one of Gandhi's great nonviolent marches he abruptly called a halt and disbanded the protest. His lieutenants came to him and said, "Mahatma, you can't do this, this act of civil disobedience has been planned for a long time, and there are too many people involved." Gandhi's reply was: "My friends, my commitment is to truth as I see it each day, not to consistency!"

Freethinkers are re-thinkers, neither afraid to take sides nor reluctant to change sides. No tradition, no revelation, no privileged knowledge lies beyond question or critical examination. There is only experience to be interpreted in the light of further experience.

Colleague Walter Royal Jones tells of the evangelist who took up her place at a busy intersection, almost hidden between the panels of a sandwich sign that proclaimed on the front in huge letters: "THE ANSWER!" The rest of the placard was blank except for these words at the bottom in small, almost inconspicuous print: (*please see the other side*). People who stopped to read the front almost always looked behind, where to their amazement, they found the identical announcement: "THE ANSWER!" with (*please see the other side*) written at the bottom.

Perplexed, some people raced from front to back then back to front and round again, while the evangelist stood there quietly. Other individuals shrugged their shoulders and left, tapping their heads as if the evangelist were a nut! Some began to snicker and left laughing. The evangelist was a clown! Still others, sensing a slight to their settled convictions, left scowling. The evangelist was a false prophet, a deceiver!

At length a wise woman came by, considered the sign from the front, then from the rear, and stood a while, pondering. Finally, she spoke. "Yes," she said, quietly, "we all want the answer, yet being willing to see another side is the only way to even come close." And the evangelist smiled approvingly.

As a community of freethinking mystics with hands Unitarian Universalists urge people of all ages in our religious home to share honest confusions as well as firm convictions. We don't bask in quandaries, but we aren't timid to confess them. In the intrepid sharing of bewilderment among trusted spiritual kin, we garner both enlightenment and resolve.

Opening our souls to variant perspectives means listening deeply rather than either posturing or pontificating. When Michelangelo painted the Sistine Chapel, he included both the major and minor prophets from the Jewish heritage. How can you tell them apart? Though cherubim appear at the ears of all, only the major prophets are listening. In true dialogue we not only seek to convince the other of our position but, more important, we allow ourselves the possibility of being persuaded by them.

The Reverend David Bumbaugh composed a poignant benediction that conveys the vision of creating a cohesive community of open-minded people:

> May our church be dedicated to the proposition that beneath all our differences, and behind all our diversity there is a unity that makes us one and binds us forever together in spite of time and death and the space between the stars. Let us pause in silent witness to that unity.

Life-Affirming Religion

Where do I wind up theologically? I don't find any label I like. You might call me a "life-affirming" mystic, with an ethic based on reverence for our oneness in the patterned energy we severally incarnate.

—Josiah Bartlett
"Odyssey"

Unitarian Universalism is unabashedly a life-affirming religion. It remains dubious about other realms but is resoundingly affirmative about the wondrous prospects presented during our earthly voyage.

During the course of our pilgrimage, it is imperative that we learn to offer at times a clear-cut No, not merely a Maybe or passive-aggressive Yes. For Unitarian Universalists dwell in the Protestant tradition, comprising those courageous women and men who have opposed injustice and combated evil. However, while denouncing wrongdoing, we must also delineate the righteous path, for protesters are literally those who "testify on behalf of" something they cherish.

Despite the inestimable value of saying No in the name of holy resistance, we remain fundamentally a

Yea-saying religion. In the midst of whatever doubts, frailties, and ambivalences life submits, our heritage tenders the most determined Yes we can humanly muster. We are loathe to follow in the footsteps of those pioneers who had valiant intentions but minimal persistence and whose epitaphs read: "Died of discretion!"

In any case, there is no way we can live consistently emboldened lives of Yes under our own spiritual steam. We need religious community to assist us in converting our convictions into commitments. We hanker for comrades who dare to lift us when we're dragging, calm us when we're hassled, deter us from a seductive No or a tempting Maybe when a hard Yes is requisite.

An old Egyptian myth teaches a valuable lesson about joy and the purpose of life. After death, Egyptians believed they would be confronted by the god Osiris with a quiz that had to be answered honestly. After forty-two routine questions concerning how the deceased had lived, Osiris asked a crucial two-part question: First, did you *find* joy? And second, did you *bring* joy?

Note that the emphasis is not on what we produce or on our possessions, not even on our creative talents or our good works. The purpose of our earthly journey according to Egyptian religion is simply this: Did you *find* joy and did you *bring* joy during your earthly sojourn? The petitioners couldn't lie to Osiris, and much was at stake. If they answered these questions affirmatively, they were returned a measure of continued existence. If not, they were taken away and forthwith eaten by a hippopotamus.

Unitarian Universalist religion claims that each of us can make a significant difference in the ongoing creation. We consider it a sin to stay mired in earnestness or succumb to melancholy. The source of unalloyed joy is planted deep within every one of our souls, if we but visit and unleash its power.

A Talmudic tale reminds us that when Moses struck the Red Sea with his wand nothing happened. The waters opened only when the first person plunged in. Indeed, in risking the first step, in taking the plunge, in venturing an unequivocal Yes to life, the seas of our days open wide.

Responsible Freedom

> I have come to be very grateful for the balanced marriage of cerebral searching and loving affirmation that is Unitarian Universalism.
>
> —Lola E. Peters
> *Soulful Journeys: The Faith of*
> *African American Unitarian Universalists*

Our religion is bristling with paradoxes, multiple truths that supplement and sharpen each other: God-fearing humanism, freethinking mystics, doubting believers, to name but a few. Responsible freedom is yet another. The Latin word *liber* (from which liberty and liberation stem) means "free." We are indeed a liberal, even liberating, faith, but not a libertarian one.

Freedom furnishes the means to pursue our bedrock human purpose: the building of the redemptive community where freethinking mystics with hands can flourish. But freedom per se doesn't necessarily get us there. It often takes us on wild goose chases or lures us into blind alleys. Freedom is the condition, not the substance, of truth. Being responsibly free is our objective. Freedom is, as Martin Buber wrote, "the run before the jump, the tuning of the violin, the possibility of communion. Independence is a foot-bridge, not a dwelling-place."

As a result, our UUA Principles declare allegiance to "a free and responsible search for truth and meaning." Ours is a *responsible* and *responsive* faith that draws from the "Jewish and Christian teachings which call us to *respond* to God's love by loving our neighbors as ourselves."

Thus, the cardinal truth of Unitarian Universalism is not that we are free, autonomous creatures but that we have been created for intimacy, for linking with others, for bonds. To be free *from* slaveries of all kinds is essential, but to be free *for* community is the mark of religious maturity. Faith, hope, and love are undeniably relational experiences. Even solitude is prelude to solidarity.

Unitarian Universalists are adamant that freedom without responsibility winds up in chaos and that responsibility without liberty results in blind obligations. The combination of responsibility plus freedom is who we are and how we choose to travel. Playwright Lillian Smith put it aptly: "Freedom and responsibility are like Siamese twins: They die if they are parted!"

Responsible freedom also entails acknowledging that every significant human relationship, institution, and cause has a price tag. Liberal religion *costs*. The stable, consequential covenants in our lives are not free. Getting something for little or nothing holds no enticement for Unitarian Universalists. Enterprises that offer free rides prove fraudulent in the long run.

As freethinking mystics with hands, we are stewards of our mutual resources. A steward is literally "a keeper of the hall." Stewards know it takes many hands to sustain a vigorous church community: hands to uphold each other, hands to maintain church property, hands to nurture offspring, and hands to spread our common faith.

We all recognize the stewards of our churches. They are the givers, not the hoarders or takers. They are the institutionalists who maintain allegiance to their chosen religious community despite personal regrets or dislikes. When there is a financial bind, stewards are generous responders. When a congregational meeting is convened, stewards stay to the bitter end. When strangers arrive at the church door, the hands of stewards are gladly extended.

Stewards do not spectate on the sidelines during church conflicts, believing they are answerable for only their portion of congregational character. Stewards contend that staying clean in the midst of messy struggles is not heroic but irresponsible behavior. They engage in whatever affectionate combat is necessary to keep the fires crackling at their religious hearth.

Nearing the close of the twentieth century, we are keenly aware that the rich and resourceful tradition of "freethinking mystics" lies in our very hands. As Max Kapp elegantly phrases it:

Many are the windows that will stay darkened unless we light them. It is our watch now! Come great hearts, come dreamers and singers and poets, come builders, come healers, come activists, come those of the soil and those who command the might of machines. Carry the sacred flame to make light the windows of the world. It is we who must be keepers of the flame. It is we who must carry the imperishable fire. It is our watch now! It is our watch now!

Semper Reformanda

The miracle of Exodus is not whether or not the Red Sea parted. That is nothing more than a poetic conceit. The miracle of Exodus is that a group of people finally realized for themselves, for us, and for all time that you cannot stay in Egypt. Any personal commitment that is not toward growing and changing, any religious commitment that is not toward goals beyond one's own personal welfare, is a commitment toward slavery in Egypt.

—John Hays Nichols
A Biblical Humanist Companion

Basically I believe I am a work in progress and as I evolve I keep cleaning house, ridding myself of old thinking, habits, and beliefs that no longer serve my current life. In essence, I try to make room for new ways of thinking and acting, feeling and being. Some I adopt and some I reject. But the end result is that I keep evolving.

—Betty Boone
"My Spiritual Home"

"Semper reformanda" was the rallying cry of the sixteenth-century Transylvanian Unitarian Francis Dávid, and it was seconded by the affirmation of modern-day Unitarian poet e. e. cummings who mused: "we can never be born enough." Our Unitarian Universalist web is permeable and fluid rather than tight or set. We belong to a springy venture, not a static organization. Unitarian Universalism is anchored to no single moment, no particular guru, no one pledge, but instead is linked to countless events, persons, and scriptures.

What does being born again mean to Unitarian Universalists? It signifies that we find gradual transformation preferable to sudden conversion. We experience turning points in our lives, but they rarely occur in a vacuum. We believe that spiritual maturity doesn't happen overnight, when we're down on our knees, feeling ecstatic or miserable. We don't get faith suddenly; we grow it progressively. In fact we don't get anything of lasting importance suddenly. Maybe thrills, some release, occasional highs, but not transformative meaning. The profundities of the religious life emerge slowly.

In addition, religious growth usually comes with considerable agonizing and upheaval. We must die in order to be reborn. Whenever struggle is replaced by sedate doctrines, our soul goes flat. As the Reverend A. Powell Davies put it:

> When someone asks where now is thy God, we can answer that the sacred is where it al-

ways was: in the struggle. In the pain of our hearts, in the growing clearness of our minds, in the sharpening edge of conscience, in the welling up of courage, in the purpose we cannot forsake and never shall.

So, we Unitarian Universalists hold our beliefs with care and responsibility, with fervor yet lightheartedness; we are editing our odysseys continuously. When Emerson was an old man, he preached for nearly two years as an interim minister at the East Lexington, Massachusetts, church using the sermons he had delivered as a young man at the Second Church in Boston. It is reported that as Emerson read the sermons, he would now and then pause, look up, and with a smile say, "I no longer believe that," and go back to reading his text. Such is the nature of Unitarian Universalist religion. It is an unfolding faith in which we often adjust or abandon yesterday's tenets.

Examples abound. A lifelong layperson says: "I started as a Universalist Christian, followed by agnosticism, then naturalistic theism. Now at the close of my journey I'm a religious humanist, yet I never had to leave Unitarian Universalism. Hallelujah!" In 1830, William Ellery Channing, when told by an acquaintance, "You seem to be the only young man I know," replied, "Always young for liberty, I trust!" And one seventeen year old writes: "Growing up Unitarian Universalist is like searching for your head, finding it, picking it up, screwing it on, having it fall off again and again, with hopes of a tighter fit next time!"

All these Unitarian Universalists hold one thing in common: our pivotal principle of *semper reformanda*—"always evolving." They exemplify the renewability of human beings. They demonstrate that we are born repeatedly throughout an entire lifetime, then we die somewhere in the middle of our drama, still maturing, ready to be born yet again in ways beyond our imagining.

Credo

If I could give you one key, and one key only,
to more abundant life, I would give you a
sense of your own worth, an unshakable sense
of your own dignity as one grounded in the
source of the cosmic dance, as one who plays
a unique part in the unfolding of the story of
the world. . . . Secure in the sense of our own
worth, we can rejoice in the worth of others
and love out of fullness instead of an inner
emptiness that eats others alive.

—Greta W. Crosby
Tree and Jubilee

Throughout Unitarian and Universalist histories we have
been intrepid enough to venture statements of "things
commonly believed among us." We have done so without ever demanding that these corporate statements
serve as creedal tests for membership. Our declarations,
while inviting general sympathy and support, always contain "liberty clauses," that is, ample room for disclaimer
and dissent. True to Unitarian Universalist form, our most
recent statement of Principles and Purposes (adopted
in 1985) will be modified or replaced in due course.

Even though our affirmations are constantly re-fined through critical dialogue with religious compan-ions, you and I remain the final determiners of who we are, what we believe, and where we're headed. To *affirm* something means both to assert and to validate it. We make something firm by declaring, then doing, it. W. H. Auden frames it similarly: "May I, composed of eros and dust, beleaguered by the same negation and despair, show an affirming flame." The primary assign-ment of Unitarian Universalist education, worship, and witness is to help people become "affirming flames."

I have grown partial to the term *credo*, because it denotes not merely intellectual accord but also giving one's loyalty or heart to something or someone in whom one believes. So, here is a collection—not ex-haustive but evocative—of affirmations that comprise the credo I try to follow.

I believe that the religious quest is an exquisite bal-ancing act wherein each day I satisfy my body, mind, heart, soul, and conscience with wholesome nutrients. We exist to employ our total selves.

I believe that laughter is life's saving grace. As George Bernard Shaw reminds us: "We need ever-deeper wisdom and ever-broader compassion; laugh-ter lubricates the job." Without humor we are joyless crusaders. We must also negotiate the fine line between being serious and being grim.

I believe that a modicum of stress is intrinsic to the religious trek. The popular quest to lead pressure-free lives is undesirable and futile. It produces spiritual zombies. Authentic religion requires periods of both peace and unrest.

I believe that roughly 30 percent of every day could be profitably spent in sheer grieving. "Blessed are they who mourn for they shall be comforted." Not only comforted, but often cleansed and fortified enough to be effective healers.

I believe that the ethical and sociopolitical struggles of life seldom allow us to escape unsullied. Customarily, we share tainted knowledge, perform imperfect deeds, and establish clumsy coalitions composed of sweethearts as well as malcontents. To compound matters, there always exists some goodness in all of our foes.

I believe that relationality is religion's primary paradigm, insinuating that wisdom is uncovered not in me or in you but *between* us—in possibilities that include yet transcend us both.

I believe that there are four interlocking and overlapping loves in life that must be equally and constantly cultivated: love of self, neighbor, the natural world, and divine mystery. Corollaries: (1) Love exists only in action; and (2) loving up-close furnishes life's most rugged chore.

I believe, along with Ben Jonson, that "Courage is the primary virtue," because unless we are brave, we won't even leave the dugout to step out on the field, let alone play ball. Cowards simply refuse to be lovers or leaders, peace-makers or justice-builders.

I believe in commitment to relationships and values over the long haul. Life belongs to the plodders, not to the speed merchants. To use a biblical metaphor, we need to run and not grow weary, but knowing that we will fatigue, we must stay awake, maintain trust, and anticipate the gracious gift of second winds.

I believe in growing old as naturally and gracefully as possible, and along with George Orwell, I observe that "everyone has the face they deserve." My brows, chin, nose, hair color, wrinkles, blemishes, and nicks—my face is mine. Not always happy, frowning when necessary, seldom hiding when in view, may it be a true face, one that reveals my genuine feelings and one that can be met head on.

Rest Assured

Death, suffering, and brevity negate life's meaning only if one assumes that a life must be long and pain-free to be worthwhile. But if life's meaning is inherent in life itself, then how long any one life is or how one suffers cannot contradict that meaning.

—Mark de Wolfe
"Living with Courage in the Face of Death"

We cannot save, be saved, but we can stand before each presence with gentle heart and hand.

—May Sarton
"A Hard Death"

If anyone wants to gain a clear grasp of Unitarian Universalist religion, attending one of our memorial services is probably the quickest way to do so. The bereaved weep, laugh, and rejoice openly, paying full homage through song, silence, and spoken words. The deceased, rather than doctrine, is center stage. The odyssey of each unique "freethinking mystic with hands" is lovingly recounted through dignified, truthful details.

The lessons of living and dying are intertwined. We believe that the pursuit of wisdom, as Socrates puts it, essentially entails the practice of dying: learning how to let go of issues and possessions, shedding illusions, pruning regrets, dropping grudges, saying farewell to our dearest notions and closest ties. We practice some dying every day, so that when we reach our physical end, we will be in reasonably good spiritual shape and with Pope John be able to declare: "My bags are packed, and I am ready to go!"

This brings to mind an instructive, yet poignant story by theologian Peter Fleck about his oldest daughter. At the age of five, she had told her four-year-old sister, who had anxiously inquired about dying: "It's nothing to be afraid of. It's just as if you were invited somewhere, and it's getting late and you go to the hostess and you say, 'Thank you for the wonderful party, I really enjoyed myself, but now it is time to go home.'" As Unitarian Universalists, we conclude that the home to which we ultimately return is serene and abundant with love. No other details are furnished or needed.

Beyond this central Unitarian Universalist principle about resting assured in the presence and aftermath of death, there are some additional suppositions we hold in common.

We believe that dying is sometimes the natural conclusion of life, at other times a premature break, but in every case, death occurs within the sweep of continuous life. To the extent that our lives are immersed in compassion and justice, our lives outlast our deaths. As Norman Cousins put it: "Our passport to immortality, to be valid, must have the stamp of the human community upon it." Therefore, our lives will be measured by whether our contributions have transcended ego gratification and served the universal good.

Lest we get carried away with self-importance, at some point memories of our singular character will become confused, even fade. Descendants will turn to more pressing matters, those who knew us personally will die. Eventually, our identity and accomplishments will shrink in stature.

Nonetheless, Unitarian Universalists believe in another facet of immortality, in the mystical sense that life returns to life. Our individual souls are reabsorbed into the eternal "Oversoul," to use Emerson's term for God. The distinctive life-energy we incarnated during our earthly sojourn flows back to the center of Creation. Cosmic life is altered because we existed.

Accordingly, we affirm that everyone is worth being cradled and caressed—remembered throughout our mortal homestretches. Even the most ordinary among us has left behind something remarkable and merits a closing tribute. For when a human being dies, a world dies, a small but distinct creation all its own, dies.

To make our final exits with sufficient integrity, gracefulness, and honor requires help from our dear comrades, including support from our faith community. Dying-with-dignity is rarely a solitary adventure. We can never overestimate the value of the *familiar*: family, friends, and surroundings. The biblical phrase for dying is apt—"to be gathered to one's people."

The grounds at my church possess a beautiful memorial garden, fountain, and wall. Sometimes I wander about the patio by myself, especially when it's quiet and uncluttered. I sit pensively and reflect a while on death in general and my own death in particular.

Staring at the memorial wall, I peruse the names of the countless friends Carolyn and I have buried as parish ministers in our two decades in San Diego. Irrepeatable individuals snuffed out at the beginning, the middle, and the close of their journeys. Tears stream down my cheeks. I also note the names inscribed on these magnificent terra-cotta plaques of persons who died before our arrival. We share a mystical yet palpable bond since Unitarian Universalism alone has drawn us to this site as spiritual relatives. In every instance, each plaque reveals but name and date, nothing puffier than that, and I am cognizant that death is truly an equalizer.

Finally, my eyes fall upon six particular plaques, four empty and two filled, all touching one another. These markers represent my parents and parents-in-law, my wife and myself. I rise from the seated bench, and I bow in permanent gratitude that, when my time to die comes, my name will be sealed on a wall alongside precious family members and dear friends, on ground we deemed sacred.